Truth and Reconciliation

by

Etan Frankel

FOUNDED 1830
NEW YORK HOLLYWOOD LONDON TORONTO
SAMUELFRENCH.COM

Copyright © 2008 by Etan Frankel
ALL RIGHTS RESERVED

CAUTION: Professionals and amateurs are hereby warned that *TRUTH AND RECONCILIATION* is subject to a royalty. It is fully protected under the copyright laws of the United States of America, the British Commonwealth, including Canada, and all other countries of the Copyright Union. All rights, including professional, amateur, motion picture, recitation, lecturing, public reading, radio broadcasting, television and the rights of translation into foreign languages are strictly reserved. In its present form the play is dedicated to the reading public only.

The amateur live stage performance rights to *TRUTH AND RECONCILIATION* are controlled exclusively by Samuel French, Inc., and royalty arrangements and licenses must be secured well in advance of presentation. PLEASE NOTE that amateur royalty fees are set upon application in accordance with your producing circumstances. When applying for a royalty quotation and license please give us the number of performances intended, dates of production, your seating capacity and admission fee. Royalties are payable one week before the opening performance of the play to Samuel French, Inc., at 45 W. 25th Street, New York, NY 10010.

Royalty of the required amount must be paid whether the play is presented for charity or gain and whether or not admission is charged.

Stock royalty quoted upon application to Samuel French, Inc.

For all other rights than those stipulated above, apply to: The William Morris Agency, LLC, 1325 Avenue of the Americas, New York, NY 10019 Attn: Val Day

Particular emphasis is laid on the question of amateur or professional readings, permission and terms for which must be secured in writing from Samuel French, Inc.

Copying from this book in whole or in part is strictly forbidden by law, and the right of performance is not transferable.

Whenever the play is produced the following notice must appear on all programs, printing and advertising for the play: "Produced by special arrangement with Samuel French, Inc."

Due authorship credit must be given on all programs, printing and advertising for the play.

ISBN 978-0-573-66035-1   Printed in U.S.A.   #22319

No one shall commit or authorize any act or omission by which the copyright of, or the right to copyright, this play may be impaired.

No one shall make any changes in this play for the purpose of production.

Publication of this play does not imply availability for performance. Both amateurs and professionals considering a production are strongly advised in their own interests to apply to Samuel French, Inc., for written permission before starting rehearsals, advertising, or booking a theatre.

No part of this book may be reproduced, stored in a retrieval system, or transmitted in any form, by any means, now known or yet to be invented, including mechanical, electronic, photocopying, recording, videotaping, or otherwise, without the prior written permission of the publisher.

IMPORTANT BILLING AND CREDIT REQUIREMENTS

All producers of *TRUTH AND RECONCILIATION* must give credit to the Author of the Play in all programs distributed in connection with performances of the Play, and in all instances in which the title of the Play appears for the purposes of advertising, publicizing or otherwise exploiting the Play and/or a production. The name of the Author *must* appear on a separate line on which no other name appears, immediately following the title and *must* appear in size of type not less than fifty percent of the size of the title type.

Winner of the 2006 L. Arnold Weissberger Award

(A light on **BEATRIZ** *[early 20's, beautiful].)*

BEATRIZ. Among the Maya there is a legend of a princess who loved a man she was not allowed to love. The two were forced to separate, but were unable to live without one another. Heartbroken, the princess visited a shaman who, moved by her sorrow, turned her into a beetle that sparkled as if covered in gems – *a piece of living jewelry.* Her lover then pinned her to his heart, so she could be with him forever.

*(***BEATRIZ** *is gone. lights up on:*

The kitchen of the Montgomery home, a tasteful, upper-middle class home in a suburb of Washington, D.C. It is 1998. It is 2PM. **LYNNE** *Montgomery (55) is seated at the table, enveloped by a sense of emptiness. She wears a dirty business suit.*

She reads from "Hansel and Gretel." Then puts the book down.)

LYNNE. *(smiles, recalling)* God you loved that part.

(Her smile fades. She takes a small tape player off the table in front of her. She sits with it. After a moment, she presses play.)

TAPE PLAYER. *(Lynne and Benjamin Sr.'s voices)* Hi, you've reached the Montgomerys, please leave us a message. *(beep; then Ben's voice – it sounds far away)* Mom, it's Ben – are you there? ...no? Okay. This is costing me a fortune so I'll be quick, my plane gets in at uhh... 6PM, at Dulles so...could you pick me up? What am I saying, of course you will...It's been, yeah it's been something and I have something to show you. It's wonderful. I can't wait....See you – wow, I'll see you tomorrow. *(beat)* Love you. *(click)*

*(***LYNNE** *rewinds the tape and plays it again.)*

TAPE PLAYER. *(Lynne and Benjamin Sr.'s voices)* Hi, you've reached the Montgomerys, please leave us a message. *(beep; then Ben's voice – it sounds far away)* Mom, it's Ben – are you there? ...no? Okay. This is costing me a fortune so I'll be quick, my plane gets in at uhh... 6PM, at Dulles so...could you pick me up? What am I saying, of course you will...It's been, yeah it's been something and I have something to show you. It's wonderful. I can't wait....See you – wow, I'll see you tomorrow. *(beat)* Love you. *(click)*

(**LYNNE** *just stares into space.*)

LYNNE. *(repeating the last words)* Love you...

(Just then: the sound of a door opening.)

BENJAMIN SR. Lynne?

LYNNE. *(surprised)* In here –

(**LYNNE** *hides the tape player.*)

LYNNE. What are you doing home? It's the middle of the afternoon –

(**BENJAMIN SR.** *comes in, stops when he sees her in the dirty clothes.*)

BENJAMIN SR. Do you want to explain yourself?

LYNNE. That's a hell of a way of saying hello.

BENJAMIN, SR. Terry Fuller called me at work.

LYNNE. Oh, so I'm back in 3rd grade and you're Dad getting a call from my teacher.

BENJAMIN SR. He was concerned about you. On top of that, he was expecting you. You told them you were going back to work today.

LYNNE. *You* told them I was going back to work today.

BENJAMIN SR. Why is your briefcase by the bannister, in the same place I left it this morning? You said you just wanted to get through the holidays and then...it's time, Lynne.

LYNNE. I had cleaning...

BENJAMIN SR. *Urgent* cleaning? Please. What happened to Pilar?

LYNNE. I was cleaning *upstairs.*

BENJAMIN SR. *(getting it)* In the attic...

LYNNE. Yes. Straightening up. There's a lot up there.

BENJAMIN SR. Dirt, apparently.

LYNNE. Ben's things are in the attic, his childhood things.

BENJAMIN SR. So is this it, then? You're going to spend your days playing with Ben's old toys and reading children's books? Perhaps you could write one yourself.

LYNNE. Benjamin, please...

BENJAMIN SR. No – really – you did get a master's in literature.

LYNNE. That was Hawthorne. This is a witch with a candy house.

BENJAMIN SR. Lynne, I think you're avoiding the discussion –

LYNNE. Which is what?

BENJAMIN SR. Which is, you haven't been to the office in *how* long now? To just give up your career like that... you were one of the best lobbyists on the Hill...*(beat)* Look – can we just clean out the attic, Lynne? Can we just clean it out and –

LYNNE. Clean it out?

BENJAMIN SR. It would be for the best. You don't need to be looking at those things.

LYNNE. We're not cleaning out the attic.

BENJAMIN SR. It would be easier for you that way. To go back to work. To concentrate.

LYNNE. *I don't want to concentrate.*

BENJAMIN SR. Why are you making this so difficult?

LYNNE. How could you think that removing those things would be for the best? Why would you do that?

BENJAMIN SR. I'm just...I'm *trying,* Lynne...can't you see that?

LYNNE. I'm trying, too, can't you see *that?*

(*Beat.*)

BENJAMIN SR. I don't like to fight. I don't like long days and coming home and fighting with you.

LYNNE. In the old days, after a quarrel, we'd go away for the weekend...

BENJAMIN SR. This is a bad weekend.

LYNNE. (*some anger*) I wasn't *asking*, I was making a *comment*.

BENJAMIN SR. (*giving up*) Fine...fine then. I'm going to go grade midterms.

(*He exits. The phone rings.* **LYNNE** *does not pick it up. It rings again. She seems oddly frightened of the phone.* **BENJAMIN SR.** *returns, looks at her quizzically, finally goes to the phone, which is near her.*)

BENJAMIN SR. Hello? / (*an immediate shudder*) Bishop Melinda, hello, I wasn't expecting – / Can you hold a moment please, Bishop? (*to* **LYNNE**) Bishop Melinda called this morning? *Twice?*

LYNNE. He left messages.

BENJAMIN SR. You didn't pick up? Wait – is that why...?

(*He doesn't need to finish the question. One look tells him it is.*)

BENJAMIN SR. He hasn't called in three years, Lynne, it must be important. (*into phone*) Bishop, sorry, miscommunication. One more moment, please. (*to* **LYNNE**) Have you lost your mind? Why didn't you call me?

LYNNE. I'm afraid of what he'll say, Benjamin.

BENJAMIN SR. We know what he's going to say. Now will you pick up the other phone?

LYNNE. We don't know what he's going to say.

BENJAMIN SR. Lynne, don't be like this. We've known from the beginning.

LYNNE. What if...isn't there a chance?

BENJAMIN SR. (*into phone*) Please accept my apologies, Bishop. If we had been aware of course we would have –

*(A light comes up on **BISHOP MELINDA** [70], seated in his office. He is Central American.)*

BISHOP MELINDA. *(on the phone)* Mr. Montgomery, please do not apologize. I am only pleased we can talk now.

BENJAMIN SR. I trust you're well.

BISHOP MELINDA. As can be expected at my age. And Mrs. Montgomery?

BENJAMIN SR. She's here, next to me.

BISHOP MELINDA. I think you both should hear what it is that I have to say.

BENJAMIN SR. I understand. *(to **LYNNE**)* He wants you to be on, too.

*(**LYNNE** shakes her head.)*

BENJAMIN SR. *(stern)* Lynne. Get on the phone.

*(**LYNNE** picks up another phone, a cordless, and stands beside her husband.)*

BISHOP MELINDA. Mrs. Montgomery?

*(**LYNNE** can't find any words. **BENJAMIN SR.** stares daggers at her and she manages –)*

LYNNE. Bishop.

BENJAMIN SR. What is it, Bishop?

BISHOP MELINDA. I have something I must speak to you both about.

BENJAMIN SR. Is it Ben?

BISHOP MELINDA. Yes.

LYNNE. *(emotional)* Is he...is he alive?

BISHOP MELINDA. I'm sorry.

*(**LYNNE** slowly drops the phone. **BENJAMIN SR.** closes his eyes, his chin tightens. Always holding in. Long pause.)*

BENJAMIN SR. So...it's definitive then.

BISHOP MELINDA. I'm afraid so.

*(**LYNNE** is crying now, the phone by her side.)*

BISHOP MELINDA. My heart goes out to both of you. *(beat)* Mrs. Montgomery?

(**BENJAMIN SR.** *awkwardly puts an arm around her – it has been some time since he has offered such a gesture and she cries even harder, possibly because the gesture reminds her of how long it has been.*)

BENJAMIN SR. She's...here. Beside me. *(beat)* Did you...find Ben's body?

BISHOP MELINDA. Not yet.

BENJAMIN SR. Then how...?

BISHOP MELINDA. Mr. Montgomery, there have been many changes in Cartuga... positive changes I'm happy to say.

BENJAMIN SR. Yes, we've read in the paper.

BISHOP MELINDA. The new government has asked me to head a commission that has been created to investigate and report on our recent history.

BENJAMIN SR. *(to* **LYNNE***)* Are you okay...?

LYNNE. Is he gone?

BENJAMIN SR. We knew he was gone.

LYNNE. But...

(She doesn't know what to say.)

BISHOP MELINDA. Mr. Montgomery, I would like to speak with you and your wife about the commission...I was wondering if it might be possible for you to fly down to Cartuga. This weekend.

BENJAMIN SR. Bishop, with all due respect, we spent quite a bit of time in Cartuga trying to find our son. We have no desire to go back.

LYNNE. Wait – what does he want?

BENJAMIN SR. He wants us to fly to Cartuga this weekend. It's about the commission.

LYNNE. *(gets on her phone)* Bishop, why do you want us to go to Cartuga?

BISHOP MELINDA. Mrs. Montgomery, as you know, for many years the citizens of this country were the victims of an army that exercised unchecked control. Thank God in heaven these people no longer have the power to terrorize. We are on a new path, a path of peace, but in order to do that we must first face our past. And that necessitates facing very ugly things. The Cartuga Truth and Reconciliation Commission is modeled on a similar commission from South Africa, and like that one it will be open to the public, for all to see, so that we as a country may heal. We must find the truth behind what happened.

LYNNE. Yes...that would mean so much...to know why....

BISHOP MELINDA. The only way to move forward is to first know the past. I am asking you to come here – to take part in the commission.

BENJAMIN SR. Take part? You don't need us.

BISHOP MELINDA. But we do. All of us – we are all trying to heal. I know it is asking a great deal, the commission would always be in your debt. But I think this very commission is the kind of thing your son lived for... and died for. Maybe this can be his legacy. Please.

BENJAMIN SR. I don't think so –

(But LYNNE *grabs* BENJAMIN SR., *looks at him, her face clearly expressing her desire to go.)*

BENJAMIN SR. Lynne. You can't be serious.

LYNNE. I think we should.

BENJAMIN SR. We're not going back there.

LYNNE. We need to go there. We need to find out why Ben was taken from us.

BENJAMIN SR. We know why. The Cartugan army kidnapped him.

LYNNE. But why? He was just a doctor, helping peasants get medical attention.

BENJAMIN SR. It was a tumultuous time. Chaotic. Who knows.

LYNNE. But maybe we *can* know. *(on phone)* Bishop, will you finally be able to tell us what happened?

BISHOP MELINDA. We are receiving new witnesses every day, new leads. Thankfully, we are solving the crimes of our past.

BENJAMIN SR. Hold on – are you saying you think you can find who's responsible?

BISHOP MELINDA. That is our goal.

BENJAMIN SR. But our investigations before went nowhere.

BISHOP MELINDA. I am pleased to say it is a new era. I am optimistic.

BENJAMIN SR. That's – the best news I've heard in three years.

LYNNE. Can we book a flight?

BENJAMIN SR. *(on the phone)* We'll fly down as soon as possible.

BISHOP MELINDA. Thank you.

(They hang up. Lights go out on the Bishop.)

BENJAMIN SR. I'm...sorry I yelled earlier. About the job. I didn't realize...

LYNNE. It's okay.

(Beat.)

BENJAMIN SR. I'll go upstairs and start packing.

LYNNE. I'll be up in a minute.

BENJAMIN SR. Are you okay? *(holding her)* We're going to be okay.

LYNNE. Why do you think they took him, Benjamin?

BENJAMIN SR. I don't know. But don't worry. We're going to get them.

(Lights down.)

Scene 2

(Outside the airport in Cartuga City, Cartuga – a country in Central America, between Guatemala and Belize and south of Mexico. It is 1995.)

BEN Montgomery *[28] struggles with three suitcases that are weighing him down. He is handsome and unpretentious.*

He approaches a car whose driver is lying on its trunk, smoking.)

BEN. Excuse me.

*(The driver [***CESAR***] looks at* **BEN**.*)*

BEN. *(struggling with Spanish)* Ex-cuse...neccesito...ummm... tu hables ingles?

CESAR. *Si, hablo ingles.*

BEN. Oh...great. Umm...I need to get to a place called uhh...here on this map, Nueva Santa Isabela.

CESAR. Nueva Santa Isabela? That is four hours from Cartuga City.

BEN. Yes, I was hoping I wouldn't have to walk it.

CESAR. You have cash?

BEN. Do you take American dollars?

*(***CESAR** *enthusiastically jumps off of the cab and throws Ben's stuff in the trunk.)*

CESAR. *(gesturing to leave)* Vamanos.

BEN. Great.

*(***BEN** *gets in the back seat and* **CESAR** *starts driving.)*

CESAR. So you from United States?

BEN. Yeah, Washington.

CESAR. Ah. Capital, yes.

BEN. How long have you lived in Cartuga?

CESAR. All my life.

BEN. In Cartuga City?

CESAR. No, I grow up in Talaca, *en el norte*.

BEN. What's it like in Nueva Santa Isabela?

CESAR. Nothing out there. Only crops and peasants. *Campesinos*.

BEN. And coffee?

CESAR. Of course.

BEN. Cartugan coffee is the best. It's all over the United States.

CESAR. Where I come from, *en el norte*, many there work the coffee beans.

BEN. What else do they farm?

CESAR. Oh, you know...there is bananas, corn, beans, sugar. Nothing up there someone from United States would like to see. Or in Nueva Santa Isabela – young man like yourself, should be in Cartuga City. Dancing... women...

BEN. I was assigned to Nueva Santa Isabela.

CESAR. What is assigned mean?

BEN. It means I was told to go there.

CESAR. You from United States, you are free, people do not tell you where to go.

BEN. I volunteered. I'm a doctor, see, and I volunteered to assist this program called Medicine Among the Nations. They go to third-world countries and provide medical assistance to – oh, I'm so sorry...I didn't mean third-world...that must sound so offensive...

CESAR. You are a doctor?

BEN. Yeah...

CESAR. No doctors in Nueva Santa Isabela.

BEN. That's why they sent me.

CESAR. Only crops and peasants out there. And *guerrilleros*.

BEN. Yes, I read about that.

CESAR. Some of them hide out there. In the hills.

BEN. I was told it was just skirmishes, it's not a war or anything. Anyway, just because there is unrest doesn't mean people should be denied medical attention, especially the most basic things.

CESAR. You are only a doctor, right?

BEN. Yeah.

CESAR. Come to Cartuga only to give medicine.

BEN. That's right.

CESAR. Nothing to worry then. Nothing to worry. Enjoy yourself. Maya ruins, go to the jungle. Maybe you see a puma, huh?

BEN. I read about those, too.

CESAR. I give you my telephone number, you need a driver anywhere I come get you.

BEN. That would be great.

CESAR. My name is Cesar.

BEN. Cesar. I'm Ben Montgomery.

CESAR. Like Montgomery Clift.

BEN. Who?

CESAR. American movie star. Montgomery Clift...?

BEN. Sorry.

CESAR. Every Saturday night, in Cartuga City, there is movies in the church. Montgomery Clift and Elizabeth Taylor, she is something...

BEN. She doesn't look so good anymore.

CESAR. Is she married?

BEN. I'm not sure...but I would imagine yes.

CESAR. Shit.

(Lights indicate a passage of time. **BEN** *looks out the window.)*

BEN. What's that?

CESAR. *Caña.* Sugar cane.

BEN. Oh. *(beat)* Did you ever work in agriculture?

CESAR. *(not understanding)* Huh?

BEN. The fields. Did you ever work in the fields?

CESAR. *(beat)* A long time ago. *(beat)* But now I own my own car, I have my own business.

BEN. That's really amazing. In my country we call that rise to success the American Dream.

CESAR. There is no dream like that here.

BEN. Oh. But then how did you do it?

CESAR. I steal.

BEN. Oh.

(BEN suddenly becomes self-conscious.)

CESAR. Do not worry, I do not steal from you.

BEN. Thank you. *(beat)* This jungle is amazing...where are the Mayan ruins?

CESAR. There is Tikal in Guatemala. Some ruins nearby and in Belize. And Mexico, of course, the Yucatan...

BEN. *(looking in his guidebook)* Right, the Yucatan.

CESAR. Here we are. Nueva Santa Isabela.

BEN. This is the whole town?

CESAR. The people here will be very happy to see you.

BEN. I hope so. I just want to get started.

CESAR. You need help with your things?

BEN. No, thank you.

(BEN hands CESAR American money.)

CESAR. Thank you.

(CESAR gives BEN a piece of paper.)

CESAR. This is my telephone number. You need a car, you call me. No one else. You call me. Okay?

(BEN takes it.)

BEN. Thanks.

(BEN gets out, takes his bags and walks off.)

CESAR. Maybe you see a puma, huh?

(CESAR watches BEN leave. Lights down.)

Scene 3

(The office of Bishop Melinda. **LYNNE** *and* **BENJAMIN SR.** *are seated, waiting silently for the Bishop. After a few moments the* **BISHOP** *enters.)*

BISHOP MELINDA. Mr. and Mrs. Montgomery.

(The **MONTGOMERYS** *rise.)*

BENJAMIN SR. Bishop Melinda, good to see you again.

(They shake hands.)

BISHOP MELINDA. So good that you could come to Cartuga. We have much to discuss. But first, your arrangements – they are satisfactory?

BENJAMIN SR. Yes, of course.

BISHOP MELINDA. If there is anything –

BENJAMIN SR. Not at all.

BISHOP MELINDA. If there is, please notify me immediately.

LYNNE. Thank you.

BISHOP MELINDA. It is so good to see you, even under these circumstances. Please sit.

(They all sit.)

LYNNE. I'm always taken aback by how lovely your country is. The trees, they look so green, so lush, from the road.

BISHOP MELINDA. Perhaps you can take a tour of the jungle and see them up close.

BENJAMIN SR. Perhaps another time.

BISHOP MELINDA. Of course.

LYNNE. Coming in from the airport, I imagine Ben must have taken that same road that we did...seen that same part of the jungle...*(beat)* We were walking here from the hotel...and I passed by a telephone and... and I couldn't help but wonder...if that was the phone Ben used to call us, to tell us that he was coming back home...and I went to pick him up at Dulles and he wasn't there...he never came...*(beat)* that message was the last time I ever heard his voice.

BISHOP MELINDA. Yes, we have new information regarding that day.

BENJAMIN SR. New information?

LYNNE. What is it?

BISHOP MELINDA. Two different sources have come forward and told us that Ben was seen in the *mercado* that day, at noon.

LYNNE. At noon?

BENJAMIN SR. But Bishop – he couldn't have been seen there at noon. Because Ben was kidnapped just before he was able to get on his 9AM flight...

BISHOP MELINDA. No, Mr. Montgomery – Ben was not yet abducted. He was seen – at the *mercado* on Calle Ramirez. At noon.

BENJAMIN SR. But – I don't understand –

LYNNE. If Ben was at the *mercado* then – why did he not get on the plane? Did he have a medical emergency or –

BISHOP MELINDA. That I do not know.

LYNNE. I was hoping we were coming here for answers, not more questions, Bishop.

BISHOP MELINDA. That is why I asked you to come.

BENJAMIN SR. To find who killed Ben.

LYNNE. Please. Don't use that word.

BENJAMIN SR. Killed? It's the truth.

LYNNE. It's cold.

BENJAMIN SR. It happened, Lynne. Okay? Can we please –

LYNNE. Don't say it like that.

BENJAMIN SR. Like what? A fact?

BISHOP MELINDA. Please. Let us remember why we are here. For your son.

LYNNE. Ben and I, we would talk about everything. And this, what happened, at the end, where he was...what he was feeling...I don't know. That is why we came,

Bishop, for you to help fill that in, to give us *that*, if nothing else.

BISHOP MELINDA. Yes, to uncover the truth...

BENJAMIN SR. So that we could put these murderers away –

BISHOP MELINDA. Well..not exactly that, Mr. Montgomery.

BENJAMIN SR. I'm sorry...? I don't understand.

BISHOP MELINDA. We are not here to put people in prison, if that is what you mean.

BENJAMIN SR. Well of course that's what I mean – what else would one do after prosecuting those responsible –

BISHOP MELINDA. Yes, but you see...we are not going to prosecute.

(Beat.)

BENJAMIN SR. But that's why you called. The Commission.

BISHOP MELINDA. I did not say prosecutions. We have come to the conclusion that a policy of amnesty is in the best interests of the nation.

BENJAMIN SR. What does that mean?

BISHOP MELINDA. We will offer amnesty to any criminal who is willing to come forward and tell us the whole truth and demonstrate that his crimes were politically motivated.

BENJAMIN SR. *(a little testy now)* Yes, but what does that *mean*, Bishop?

BISHOP MELINDA. It means that many who would hide will now volunteer to tell us everything, so that we may know the truth and build the future based on a collective memory of the past and thus create the environment for *reconciliation*.

BENJAMIN SR. Bishop, are you telling me that these people – these murderers – if they just admit to their murders then you would say thank you and let them free?

BISHOP MELINDA. Mr. Montgomery, prosecutions are lengthy and expensive. And they end up revealing very little. Would we have more in jail? Yes. Would we know what happened to your son? No. Prosecutions fail to solve the larger problems of hate and distrust. Only reconciliation can accomplish that.

BENJAMIN SR. How can you possibly pardon these murderers?

BISHOP MELINDA. A pardon is saying you excuse their crime. This is not what we are saying. Amnesty is a freedom from prosecution, not guilt.

BENJAMIN SR. What's the difference?

BISHOP MELINDA. For a nation trying to move forward, a great deal, sir.

BENJAMIN SR. Is this some kind of sick joke?

BISHOP MELINDA. Many parents lost children here in the past 40 years, Mr. Montgomery. We are all trying to heal and find a way for this never to happen again.

BENJAMIN SR. This isn't the way.

BISHOP MELINDA. There is more I must tell you.

LYNNE. What?

BISHOP MELINDA. A man who participated in your son's murder has come forward. He has applied for amnesty.

LYNNE. *(does not know how to react)* Oh dear God.

BENJAMIN SR. You – you have the man – who killed Ben?

BISHOP MELINDA. He has come forward. I wanted to tell you in person.

BENJAMIN SR. *(incredulous)* Wait a minute – Bishop, are you saying that we flew down here in order for you to tell us that you're going to give the man who murdered our son amnesty?

BISHOP MELINDA. If what he says is the whole truth...then yes.

BENJAMIN SR. Where is he?

BISHOP MELINDA. He lives outside of the capital.

BENJAMIN SR. *(insistent)* Where?

BISHOP MELINDA. I'm sorry, I cannot reveal that.

LYNNE. *(a sense of urgency)* Bishop, he's going to tell us what happened to Ben?

BISHOP MELINDA. Yes.

BENJAMIN SR. This isn't right.

LYNNE. But Benjamin –

BISHOP MELINDA. I understand your discomfort, Mr. Mont –

BENJAMIN SR. I don't think you do.

BISHOP MELINDA. Excuse me, sir, but three priests from this very church were taken and never seen again. Men I had known my whole life. So please do not minimize the pain that I, too, feel.

LYNNE. Of course we were not trying –

BENJAMIN SR. Whoever killed those priests should be hanged from a rope.

BISHOP MELINDA. More killing does not lead to peace – just to more killing.

BENJAMIN SR. This is unbelievable. I can't believe what I'm fucking *hearing* here.

LYNNE. Benjamin, please. We're in a church.

BISHOP MELINDA. There is another thing.

BENJAMIN SR. Oh Jesus Christ, what now? You buy them each a new car?

BISHOP MELINDA. As head of the commission, it is my duty to question those who seek amnesty. It is also the victim's right – or in the case of a murder, his family's right – to also question the man.

LYNNE. You mean...*we* confront him?

BISHOP MELINDA. Yes.

BENJAMIN SR. When?

BISHOP MELINDA. His session before the commission has been scheduled – it is in two days.

LYNNE. *(it hits her)* Two days?

BENJAMIN SR. Oh I'll confront him –

BISHOP MELINDA. *Verbally*, Mr. Montgomery.

LYNNE. Did you hear that? Benjamin – we'll finally *know*.

(Lights down.)

Scene 4

(Ben's examination room in the church. Faded white walls that have not been painted in many years. An old examination bed with mattress. A cross on the wall. Ben has his supplies on a desk.

BEN sits in his chair organizing his things. He looks exhausted by the day's activities. There is a knock at the door.)

BEN. Come in – I mean, oh hell what's the Spanish... ummm...

(BEATRIZ walks in. Naturally beautiful. An innocence.)

BEN. El translator...umm – tomorrow...

BEATRIZ. It is okay I come in?

BEN. *(surprised)* You speak English.

BEATRIZ. Yes.

BEN. Yes, of course, come in, please. How can I help you?

BEATRIZ. You are the one that helped Diego?

BEN. *(trying to remember)* Diego...

BEATRIZ. Little Diego...

BEN. *(remembers)* Right! Little Diego. How's he doing?

BEATRIZ. Good.

BEN. Oh, good.

BEATRIZ. You look young to be a doctor.

BEN. You look young to speak English so well.

BEATRIZ. I learned in school.

BEN. So did I. *(beat)* So...what can I help you with?

BEATRIZ. Uhh...nothing.

BEN. Then why'd you come see me?

(She turns to leave – a pain hits her in the stomach.)

BEN. If you're sick I can help you.

BEATRIZ. You are very young.

BEN. Yeah but maybe I know what I'm doing. Why don't

you give me a shot?

BEATRIZ. Give you a shot? *You* are the doctor, not me!

BEN. No – I mean, let me try. I think I can help you. I helped Diego, right?

BEATRIZ. *(still wary)* Yes...

BEN. So what is it?

BEATRIZ. My stomach...it hurts...after I eat.

BEN. Do you have loss of appetite?

BEATRIZ. What is that?

BEN. Do you not feel hungry?

BEATRIZ. Yes.

BEN. Occasional nausea...? *(BEATRIZ looks puzzled so he elaborates)* Umm – do you feel like you may get sick?

BEATRIZ. Yes.

BEN. Okay. I'd like to do a quick check. Remove your blouse please and lie down.

(She stares at him.)

BEN. Please take off your blouse and lie on the examination table so that I can take a look at you.

BEATRIZ. "Take a look at me?"

BEN. Listen, I'm a professional. This is what I do. I went to Yale, okay?!

BEATRIZ. What is Yale?

BEN. A very good school. We're in a church so you have nothing to worry about.

(BEATRIZ looks at the cross on the wall. Then removes her blouse and sits on the examination bed, in only a bra. She is shy about her body, too shy to ever contemplate the fact that she is beautiful.

BEN examines her. First he checks her heart and lungs by hearing her breathing.)

BEN. I've never practiced medicine in a church before.

BEATRIZ. It is all the town has. There is no hospital near here.

(The metal of the stethoscope is cold against her skin and

she reacts.)

BEN. Cold?

BEATRIZ. *(a yes)* Mm-hmm.

BEN. Sorry....Breathe...

(She does.)

BEN. Do you live here in Nueva Santa Isabela?

BEATRIZ. No, I go to university.

BEN. Breathe. What do you study?

(She breathes.)

BEATRIZ. I study agronomy.

BEN. What's that?

BEATRIZ. You do not know?

BEN. Afraid not.

*(***BEATRIZ** *chuckles.)*

BEN. What's so funny?

BEATRIZ. You are the one who is supposed to know English.

BEN. Alright, very funny. Make fun of the American.

BEATRIZ. Agronomy is the study of land, crops, water – how we use it best, how to organize, ummm...manage.

BEN. I guess that would be very important here, right? – breathe – Since it's such an agricultural-based society?

BEATRIZ. These people, many of them, all they know is working the land, and all their children will know is working the land so...I try to help them.

BEN. My society is so separated from working their own land – you know, that kind of self-sufficiency. But most Cartugans don't own their own land, right?

BEATRIZ. No...

BEN. So how exactly do you help them?

BEATRIZ. You ask many questions.

BEN. My mother always said I was very inquisitive.

BEATRIZ. *(suddenly self-conscious)* I...I don't want to talk.

BEN. Oh...okay. *(beat)* Once more – breathe, please. *(beat)*

So if you are at the university what do you do here in Nueva Santa Isabela?

BEATRIZ. Why do you ask these questions?

BEN. I'm new here and want to get to know Cartuga. I've read so much but you can't get the truth from a book, you have to explore and talk to people, right? – can you open your mouth?

(She does. He checks for signs of infection.)

BEN. Okay...

BEATRIZ. Why do you come here?

BEN. To offer medical help. I'm part of a program called –

BEATRIZ. *(feeling threatened)* I am just a student.

BEN. Are you alright?

BEATRIZ. Just a student at the university.

BEN. *(confused)* Umm...okay? *(beat)* Tell me if this hurts.

(He feels and pushes against parts of her belly. She reacts with pain on a couple of occasions. He stops, then hands her the blouse back, which she quickly puts back on.)

BEN. Well, looks like you've got gastritis, which is an inflammation of the lining of the stomach. I didn't see any scar tissue from burns or signs of surgery – have you been taking any drugs? Aspirin?

BEATRIZ. Yes, I take aspirin. For my headaches.

BEN. So that's probably it. Lay off the aspirin for awhile.

BEATRIZ. That is all?

BEN. Some people's stomach lining is highly sensitive to aspirin. If you don't feel better, come see me again.

(She nods. Then:)

BEATRIZ. I am just a student, okay?

BEN. You mentioned that. Are you sure you're okay?

BEATRIZ. Yes.

(She gets up.)

BEATRIZ. You leave this week?

BEN. No. I'm here for four months.

BEATRIZ. The doctors, they come for a week one time in eight months.

BEN. Yes, but I offered to be here longer.

BEATRIZ. Why?

BEN. Because I never understood how you could possibly help an entire town in one week. *(beat)* Would you like a Fanta?

BEATRIZ. You have Fanta?

BEN. Orange and Cherry.

BEATRIZ. Orange.

(He hands her a bottle of orange Fanta. He realizes he doesn't know where he left the bottle opener.)

BEN. Oh – uhhh..

(He looks around for it.)

BEATRIZ. Umm – hello?

(She pulls out of her pocket a tool like a Swiss army knife that serves different functions. She opens the Fanta.)

BEN. Oh good. I must have misplaced the bottle opener.

BEATRIZ. *(takes a sip)* Thank you, doctor...

BEN. Montgomery. Like Montgomery Clift.

(She has no idea who that is.)

BEN. Ben. Is fine.

BEATRIZ. Doctor Ben.

BEN. And you...

BEATRIZ. Beatriz.

BEN. That's a beautiful name.

*(**BEATRIZ** doesn't know what to say, starts to walk out...)*

BEN. Let me know if you don't feel better...

*(She half-nods, walks out. **BEN** watches her go.)*

Scene 5

(The Cartuga Truth and Reconciliation Commission.
LYNNE & BENJAMIN SR. *are seated.* **BISHOP MELINDA**
is addressing the room.)

BISHOP MELINDA. *Llamo hoy la seccion de la Commission de la Verdad y la Reconsilacion de Cartuga en orden. Por el beneficio de las familia de las victima, vamos a conducir la seccion de hoy en Ingles. Transmitiremos la traducion por radio.*

As we call today's session to order I know those out there listening on their radios and all those here will share in my personal grief at the loss of a visitor to our country, a young man who was taken too soon, whose legacy is this commission, and peace. A moment of silence please for Doctor Benjamin Montgomery.

*(***LYNNE & BENJAMIN SR.** *clasp hands. There is silence.)*

BISHOP MELINDA. Thank you. This morning's session presents a man confessing complicity in Dr. Montgomery's death and seeking amnesty from this commission. Will he please come forward...

*(***CESAR**, *the cab driver, comes forward. He sits before the commission. He carries himself as a man who feels no guilt – this is simply an exercise to avoid prison.*

LYNNE *puts a hand on* **BENJAMIN SR.**'*s shoulder partly to comfort him and in part to keep him from getting up and going after* **CESAR.**)

BISHOP MELINDA. *Usted necessito un translador?*

CESAR. *(proud)* I know *ingles.*

BISHOP MELINDA. Please state your name.

CESAR. Cesar Santos.

BISHOP MELINDA. And you are from...

CESAR. Talaca.

BISHOP MELINDA. And you are here to offer information?

CESAR. I am.

BISHOP MELINDA. And this will be entirely the truth?

CESAR. I go free then. No jail, yes?

BISHOP MELINDA. If you tell us all, and it is all true, and politically motivated, then yes.

CESAR. What is politically motivated?

BISHOP MELINDA. It means your crime cannot have been motivated by robbery or a petty squabble – it must be rooted in political ideology.

CESAR. Yes, this is politically motivated. So I do not go to jail.

BISHOP MELINDA. And we hope by the proceeding that you can make amends.

CESAR. *(doesn't know what it means)* Make amends?

BISHOP MELINDA. That you will mend a rift. By seeing the error of your ways.

CESAR. What error?

BISHOP MELINDA. Killing someone, you see.

CESAR. No error.

BISHOP MELINDA. Are you saying it was not wrong to kill this innocent man?

CESAR. Killing a innocent man is wrong, yes, but this man is not innocent.

BISHOP MELINDA. Are you saying he was guilty of something?

CESAR. No – he is innocent now, now we know yes, this man is innocent – but then, no, we think he is guilty. A guilty man must die, you see.

BISHOP MELINDA. Why?

CESAR. Bishop, this is what war is.

BISHOP MELINDA. But Dr. Montgomery was in Nueva Santa Isabela as a doctor –

CESAR. He is a dangerous man.

BISHOP MELINDA. Why?

CESAR. *(beat)* I am allowed a statement, yes?

BISHOP MELINDA. Yes. Usually taken at the conclusion of the inquest.

CESAR. I can take it now?

BISHOP MELINDA. If you wish.

CESAR. I wish, yes.

BISHOP MELINDA. Mr. Santos will make his statement before we continue with the inquest.

CESAR. *(beat)* I grow up in Talaca, *en el norte*. My father – he is a *campesino*, he work his fields for years, coffee beans, to export to United States. The army come in and take our land – we build this land, make it rich, so now they take it from us. What are we to do? We have no weapons, only our picks and shovels.

So we work where we can – my father, my brother Paco, me – we work where we can find, work someone else's land, some rich man's land, all day we work and take home almost nothing. And every day we pass *nuestra tierra* – our land – and I swear to this land one day we will have you back.

Los soldados – the army soldiers – they know this, our anger. One day, when my father goes to *la ciudad* for supplies, *mi hermano* – Paco – and me – we go home from work, only Paco likes to race home. He always say to me we must be in shape, be strong, ready to take back our land, you see. So at the end of the long work day he race home to show that we are strong.

Paco is fast, he reaches our home as I still climb the final hill. As I near the top of the hill I hear a gunshot. *Mi corazon...(he gestures, showing his reaction when his heart jumped)* I look over the hill to see my house. There are *soldados* there, men with guns, and they have Paco on the ground. A bullet in his leg. He is helpless. And I know why he has a bullet in his leg. It is because when he sees *los soldados* he tries to run, not to run for freedom you see, he knows this is not possible, but because he wants them to shoot him *so I will hear the gunshot*. So that I will stop and save myself. Paco...the look on his face...he knows...*que lo van a matar.*

BISHOP MELINDA. He knew he was going to die.

CESAR. I hide behind a tree, I can do nothing, as they pour gasoline on *mi casa, mi casa* where I am raised. Now Paco is on the ground and *me puede ver*, Bishop...he can see me behind the tree until the time when they put him inside our home and leave him there. Bishop, *no puedo hacer nada.* I can do nothing. That is when I run away. My hands over my ears. I do not want to see the fire burn my home. I do not want to hear Paco's screams. I run all night. *No puedo hacer nada.*

(*beat*) Later...I find my father before he comes to the remains of our home and I tell him about Paco, *mi hermano, su hijo.* But *papa* – he is dead inside already. He takes his supplies and continues down the road, *a trabajar*, work for the rich man who pays him nothing and spits on his land. Me – I cannot do this. I cannot work for this man any longer. I go to Cartuga City, work all day and night to make money, do whatever I have to get by, and I promise myself that Paco *no muere vano.* Paco does not die in vain.

(**CESAR** *takes a moment.*)

BISHOP MELINDA. What happened to your father?

CESAR. This I do not know. Perhaps he is still now working in those fields. Or perhaps he is dead like Paco.

BISHOP MELINDA. There is something I do not understand, Mr. Santos. The army does all this to you – takes all this away – and then, years later, you work for them?

CESAR. I never work for the army. I spit on the army.

BISHOP MELINDA. But – the army ordered Dr. Montgomery's murder.

CESAR. (*as if it is obvious*) No, Bishop. Not the army. It is *los guerrilleros, los guerrilleros* say the doctor must die.

(**LYNNE & BENJAMIN SR.** *are shocked.*)

LYNNE. The guerillas?

(*Lights down.*)

Scene 6

(Ben's examination room. A couple of weeks later. He looks exhausted. He is lying on the examination bed trying to steal a quick nap. There is a knock at the door. **BEATRIZ** *enters.* **BEN** *looks up.)*

BEN. *(pleasantly surprised)* Hi.

BEATRIZ. Doctor Ben.

BEN. I was wondering how you were feeling.

BEATRIZ. You are sleeping...

BEN. No – well I was – just for a minute. How is your stomach?

BEATRIZ. It still hurts.

BEN. A lot?

(She nods.)

BEATRIZ. I hope – I come here because maybe you will look again?

BEN. Sure. I'll see what I can do.

BEATRIZ. But if you are sleeping –

BEN. No, no. It's fine.

*(***BEN*** jumps off the examination bed and grabs the stethoscope.* **BEATRIZ** *removes her blouse and sits on the bed – there is nothing sexual about it, simply an expression of her comfort with him.* **BEN** *turns around and sees her sitting on the bed with no blouse on.)*

BEN. Oh – umm...okay, I guess we can get started then.

(He begins the examination. He periodically asks her to breathe.)

BEATRIZ. I asked about you.

BEN. I'm sorry, what?

BEATRIZ. In town. I asked about you.

BEN. Why?

BEATRIZ. You have been here three weeks and already you help so many people.

BEN. *(charmed)* You asked about me?

BEATRIZ. They say they have been coming from many towns to see you, some walk all morning. You are their hope.

BEN. *(a smile)* Really?

BEATRIZ. *(noticing his reaction)* What?

BEN. No, I just...felt a tinge of gratification.

BEATRIZ. Is that good?

BEN. Yes, it means I feel good. *(beat)* Turn to your left.

(*She turns to her left and he continues to examine her.*)

BEATRIZ. It is funny because...

BEN. What's funny?

BEATRIZ. One man in town thought you maybe were a spy.

BEN. *(amused)* Spy? I'm a doctor.

BEATRIZ. Spies are many things.

(*Beat.*)

BEN. So how do you know that I'm not a spy?

BEATRIZ. Because you do nothing but medicine. And you never leave this church.

BEN. I've been busy with patients.

BEATRIZ. Yes, I know.

BEN. You ask the townspeople that, too?

BEATRIZ. Yes.

BEN. Why'd you ask them all that?

BEATRIZ. Because I wanted to know why you came.

BEN. I told you.

BEATRIZ. Americans do not come to Cartuga for more than a week... unless they are CIA.

BEN. CIA?

BEATRIZ. CIA were here many times, they trained the army.

BEN. But that was years ago.

BEATRIZ. Sometimes they come again. With weapons, supplies, advice for the army...

(**BEN** *continues to examine her in silence. After a few moments, he presses against part of her belly. She does not react.*)

BEN. You aren't sick are you?

(*She sits up.*)

BEN. Not anymore.

BEATRIZ. No...

(*He hands her the blouse. She puts it on.*)

BEN. I don't understand, why are you here?

BEATRIZ. I was...curious...about you. It is not everyday that I remove clothes for a man. *(a hint of playful)* Regardless of what you hear in town... *(beat)* That was a joke. *(beat)* You asked about me also – you tell me why?

BEN. I didn't ask about you.

BEATRIZ. Diego told me.

BEN. Diego! That was supposed to fall under doctor-patient confidentiality! *(she laughs)* That's it – no more medicine for Diego.

BEATRIZ. You did not answer my question.

BEN. I guess I was curious too.

(*Beat.*)

BEN. Fanta?

BEATRIZ. Orange.

(*He goes to get her a Fanta.* **BEATRIZ** *notices a package that contained chocolate on his desk.*)

BEATRIZ. *(excited)* You have chocolate?

BEN. Oh, no, it's empty. Sorry. You like chocolate?

BEATRIZ. *(a yes)* Mm. American chocolate from the *mercado*.

BEN. Oh, so you like things from America.

BEATRIZ. *Some* things.

(*He laughs, hands her the Fanta.*)

BEATRIZ. So how is it that you are so young for a doctor?

BEN. I just recently became a doctor – just finished my residency.

BEATRIZ. You come where there is no money. Why?

BEN. Maybe I come where there is…gratification. It's just the way I was raised.

BEATRIZ. Why Cartuga?

BEN. I had a friend in grade school whose mother was Cartugan. We would go to his house after school and his mother would always fix us snacks, and she'd tell us about her homeland. The rainforests, where you could spot a puma or a jaguar roaming around, and the termites, they tasted minty she said, and I would wince and she would laugh. And I had this picture in my mind, it was so vivid and magical. So when I put my request in…I had only one picture in my head. And luckily I got the assignment.

BEATRIZ. How does it compare?

BEN. The only thing I've seen much of is the inside of this church. I sent my mother a picture of it and wrote that this is the only part of Cartuga that I know. She'll get a kick out of that. She's probably the reason I'm here.

BEATRIZ. She made you come?

BEN. *(a chuckle)* No, she didn't make me. It was my idea. But she's the reason I wanted to come. My dad thinks it's just a phase, just getting something out of my system, but my mom understands. She's this amazing socially conscious person. For years she would take me to meetings and rallies with her – human rights, women's rights, the environment. She'd always say, "Always act on your principles." I really admire her.

BEATRIZ. Is that why you are here? Because you believe in something?

BEN. I guess I believe in helping people get medicine even if they don't have money. *(correcting himself)* Especially if they don't have money.

BEATRIZ. I wish the army believed such things.

BEN. What does the army believe?

BEATRIZ. *(mocking him)* Did you not read about it in your book?

BEN. I want to know what you think.

BEATRIZ. They believe in protecting the rich. The landowners. But the students – the agronomy students – we have a responsibility – to help the peasants. It is their work that leads to coffee export to your United States. And yet – their land is taken from them by the army, they struggle to stay alive – and their leaders are made to disappear by the army intelligence, the *Informacion Central.* Even my own mentor, Carlos, is threatened.

BEN. Because he helps organize the *campesinos?*

BEATRIZ. Any challenge to the army's control is a threat. There is a van, a black van, *La Panel Negra,* that appears in our streets. When you are taken into the van you are never heard from again. They find them – the student leaders, peasant organizers…they find them and they disappear.

BEN. Jesus…

BEATRIZ. Only last week a man came to Carlos' home and told him to stop organizing the peasants or *La Panel Negra* would be at his doorstep. But he will not stop – he is too principled a man to do that. *(beat)* In the rural areas the army so fears the spread of communism, their policy is to "drain the sea to kill the fish."

BEN. What does that mean?

BEATRIZ. Communism is like a fish in a sea of people. But a fish cannot live if there is no sea to swim in, yes? So they remove the sea.

BEN. But don't the guerillas defend the peasants?

BEATRIZ. The guerillas *say* they fight for the peasants but… nobody really fights for the peasants…that is why I try to help Carlos organize them. Because a large group that is unified *is* power. That is how I try to change things.

BEN. *(beat)* You're pretty amazing.

(**BEATRIZ** *doesn't know how to react to that statement, just sips her Fanta.*)

BEN. Is it dangerous to tell me all this?

BEATRIZ. I feel like I can say things to you. Can I?

BEN. Yes. Doctor/patient confidentiality.

BEATRIZ. Good.

(*She finishes her Fanta.*)

BEATRIZ. Done.

(*She rises as if to leave...*)

BEATRIZ. You must have a great deal of work...

BEN. Actually I'm done for the day. Do you...would you like to stay?

BEATRIZ. I am not sick anymore.

BEN. You can pretend you are.

BEATRIZ. Pretend?

(**BEATRIZ** *"pretends" to have a stomach ache and sits on the examination bed.*)

BEATRIZ. Awwwww.

BEN. As your doctor I must advise you to stay until your stomach feels better.

BEATRIZ. As long as I do not have to remove my blouse.

BEN. You don't have to remove your blouse.

BEATRIZ. Whatever you say, doctor Ben.

(*lights down.*)

Scene 7

(Outside of a building in Cartuga City. **LYNNE** *stands, wearing the same skirt and blouse she wore to the commission, but not the jacket.*

BENJAMIN SR. *comes up behind her.)*

BENJAMIN SR. What are you looking at?

LYNNE. Just the buildings. They look so fragile. Benjamin – the guerillas? Why would *they* take him? He was *helping* the peasants.

BENJAMIN SR. I don't know.

(She shivers.)

BENJAMIN SR. You're cold.

LYNNE. *(a lie)* I'm okay.

BENJAMIN SR. You should probably try to get some sleep. Tomorrow's going to be a long day.

LYNNE. I haven't slept in three years, I think I know how to handle it.

BENJAMIN SR. Would you like a Valium? *(she ignores that)* You know, Dr. Markman said you could see him anytime.

LYNNE. *(dismissive)* Please...

BENJAMIN SR. He's written a number of books, Lynne. They've been well-received.

LYNNE. Grief is not something you "talk out," Benjamin. It's not a car, it doesn't depreciate over time.

BENJAMIN SR. Some things settle...even terrible things...

LYNNE. Like sending your child into the world to be kidnapped at gunpoint? Just because he believed in something?

BENJAMIN SR. Lynne –

LYNNE. I believed in something once.

BENJAMIN SR. What are you talking about?

LYNNE. I did the work I did because of *Ben*, because I wanted to change the world that he was growing up in. And then when Ben...*(beat)* disappeared...what's the point anymore? I just...it's what I always believed, it's what I taught him but I didn't know that this would happen, I...*I didn't know,* Benjamin – I didn't know I wouldn't have him forever...

*(A wave of guilt rushes over **LYNNE** and she starts to well up.)*

BENJAMIN SR. Can you please take a Valium?

*(**LYNNE** nods a yes. **BENJAMIN SR.** hands one to her, she takes it.)*

LYNNE. Do you feel *anything*? Anything at all?

*(**LYNNE** turns her gaze away from him. Beat. **BENJAMIN SR.** breathes in, then downs a Valium himself.)*

BENJAMIN SR. I'll be inside.

*(He exits. **LYNNE** pulls out the tape player she was hiding, presses play.)*

BEN'S VOICE. – and I have something to show you. It's wonderful. I can't wait....

(Click. She stops it. Shivers again. Hugs herself to stay warm.)

LYNNE. What was it you wanted to show me, Ben? Can you tell me?

*(After a moment, **BEN** appears behind her, takes off his white doctor's coat, wraps it over her shoulders. She doesn't respond to any of this – as if he's not really there – she just continues staring out. Lights down.)*

End of Act 1

ACT II

Scene 1

(Ben's examination room. He is standing by the open door talking to a noisy waiting room. He wears the white coat.)

BEN. Okay, Alvaro, remember to take that twice a day – *dos a dias. Comprendes?* Now who's next? – Señorita Santiago, I'll be with you in five minutes. *Cinco minutos.* *(beat)* I think you're next, Señorita Fuentes...how are you feeling...?

*(In walks **BEATRIZ**. There is something fake in their delivery.)*

BEATRIZ. The pain is very bad. Some days I cannot even study.

BEN. Let's take a look then.

*(**BEN** closes the door. **BEATRIZ** smiles and giggles.)*

BEATRIZ. *(flirty)* Buenas dias, doctor Ben.

BEN. *(flirty)* Buenas dias, Ms. Fuentes.

(He kisses her. They giggle like naughty schoolchildren.)

BEN. I saw you waiting there but I couldn't call you, I had to go in order or it would look suspicious.

BEATRIZ. I know...

BEN. And Señora Vasques was telling me about the pain in her leg and all I could think about was seeing you.

BEATRIZ. *(chuckling)* That explains why her leg has not improved.

BEN. It was torture.

BEATRIZ. I missed you.

BEN. It's been two days. This is really hard. Who knew two days would feel like two months.

BEATRIZ. I thought about you. In my meeting yesterday. Looking forward to today. I told my family I was going to church which is not a lie really. They think suddenly I am the best Catholic. *(beat)* I feel like the quetzal.

BEN. What's that?

BEATRIZ. The bird in our jungle. To us they symbolize freedom, because they are unable to survive in captivity. And here I am, every moment I can find, flying away to you.

(They kiss again.)

BEATRIZ. How is today?

BEN. Good. It's nice to see people feeling better. There was one patient that came in with an eye infection. That was pretty cool. And another thought he had pneumonia –

*(**BEATRIZ** sees a paper on his desk.)*

BEATRIZ. *(alarmed)* Jose Huerta?

BEN. Yeah, turned out it was just a rolling cough.

BEATRIZ. You saw Jose Huerta?

BEN. You probably shouldn't see those, they're confidential. Do you know him?

BEATRIZ. The Lieutenant?

BEN. I don't know – I didn't ask him what he does. What's wrong?

BEATRIZ. Why do you see him?

BEN. Because he came by. I examined him. What's the matter?

BEATRIZ. Lieutenant Huerta is a member of the army's anti-guerilla unit. Why would you see him?

BEN. I'm a doctor, Beatriz, I see people who aren't feeling well – that's how it works.

BEATRIZ. Have you been truthful with me?

BEN. What are you talking about?

BEATRIZ. *(frightened)* I told you so much – if you are working with Huerta or –

BEN. How can you say that? He was just here for a doctor visit.

BEATRIZ. Yes, this is the same explanation we give.

(Beat.)

BEN. Fine, this is wrong but – HERE. Read it.

(He hands her the file. She takes it, reads.)

BEN. His doctor in Cartuga City said he was fine but he wanted a second opinion, from an American he said. Beatriz, I'm not here because of politics, I'm here because I'm a doctor, that's IT. That's what I do. I'm in this room practically all day, seeing patients, I'm not involved in anything.

BEATRIZ. I am sorry.

BEN. Do you see?

*(**BEATRIZ** nods a yes.)*

BEN. I know what it's like for you here but – how can you question me like that?

BEATRIZ. You do not know what it is like. The bullets, the machetes, the vanished neighbors. When you lose people...friends...

BEN. Who have you lost...?

BEATRIZ. *(beat)* Mara. She lived in my town when I was a child. She would make sweets and give them to me when my father was not looking. Last year a guerilla soldier visited her, he asked to use her home as a safe house. She refused. She said she did not want to be involved. She only cared about raising her three children. The soldier left. Someone in town saw the soldier leave her home and the next week it was burned to the ground by the army and she was found with three bullets in her head. Only because someone saw a guerilla leave her home. That is all it takes here. A drop of suspicion. As if lives mean nothing. This is a place without shelter and without pity. Cautious is how one survives.

BEN. Beatriz, I'm so sorry. I want you to trust me.

BEATRIZ. I saw the Lieutenant's name, I reacted. This is how it is here – but it is not how we want it to be. *(beat)* I'm sorry...

BEN. Do you trust me?

BEATRIZ. Yes.

(They look at each other.)

BEATRIZ. How could I not trust those eyes.

(She touches him.)

BEATRIZ. Maybe now you see why my work is so important – by helping the peasants unite together we can change things.

BEN. I admire you.

BEATRIZ. Really?

BEN. In a strange way you remind me of my mother.

BEATRIZ. I do not know if I like that kind of strange.

BEN. *(smiling)* No. I mean your idealism. What you believe. I really think you're amazing.

BEATRIZ. I was just born here. You are the one who chose to come.

(They stare at each other for a moment.)

BEATRIZ. Now, it is time for my exam.

BEN. But you're feeling fine.

BEATRIZ. Shall I take something off?

BEN. What?

BEATRIZ. You are going to examine me, no?

BEN. Beatriz – there's something very wrong about a doctor doing this.

BEATRIZ. What, you do not like what is underneath?

BEN. Not at all, you're stunning, gorgeous – I wish I could quote Pablo Neruda or something...but there is a waiting room of people outside.

BEATRIZ. So let them wait.

BEN. They need to be looked at.

BEATRIZ. I have gastritis, yes? Attend to me.

BEN. You do not.

BEATRIZ. I did. Follow up exam?

BEN. *You* were the one who said no one could find out about us. What if they hear?

BEATRIZ. What if they do not hear?

BEN. What if you came back...tonight.

BEATRIZ. No, I could not. We must not be seen.

BEN. I know.

BEATRIZ. Still...I want to hold you in my arms tonight.

BEN. That would be beautiful.

BEATRIZ. I want to take you to the caves, a few kilometers down the path from the church, where the river flows in pitch darkness, and it is cold like the winter months. And I would wrap you in my arms, and we would lie by the mouth of the cave and sleep.

BEN. Yes...

BEATRIZ. In the morning we would bathe in the water and warm ourselves in the sun and eat chocolate until noon and then go back to sleep.

BEN. Just chocolate?

BEATRIZ. Yes, just Hershey's chocolate. My favorite. You have a problem with chocolate?

BEN. No, no. It all sounds perfect.

BEATRIZ. Perhaps...one day...

BEN. Maybe at night? Like tonight.

BEATRIZ. We could be spotted.

BEN. Maybe it would be worth the risk...

BEATRIZ. No. No risk is worth getting hurt. *(beat)* Some day though, I will get to examine you?

BEN. *(chuckles)* We'll see.

BEATRIZ. Have you...examined a girl before, Ben?

BEN. *(a smile)* That's the first time you've called me Ben without the doctor.

BEATRIZ. Have you?

BEN. Yes. Is that a problem?

BEATRIZ. No. And I like how you tell me the truth.

BEN. It doesn't matter to me if you –

BEATRIZ. I have not. Catholic.

BEN. Funny, I know lots of Catholic girls...

BEATRIZ. Were you in love?

BEN. No, never.

BEATRIZ. Why not?

BEN. I don't know. For years I watched my friends fall in and out of love like it was a pastime –

BEATRIZ. *(doesn't understand the word)* Pastime?

BEN. Like it meant nothing. But I imagined it as so much more, this kind of higher plane of emotion...maybe it's stupid but...I just always *wanted* to believe...

BEATRIZ. That is nice...

BEN. But it never happened. Not even close. Which made me wonder, because my best friend once told me that maybe love just doesn't happen that way for everyone... maybe it doesn't explode into your life...but I find that so depressing...

BEATRIZ. Do you feel explosions?

BEN. Now?

BEATRIZ. Yes.

(BEN is suddenly self-conscious, maybe letting her too close too soon. He is quiet.)

BEATRIZ. *(beat)* Because maybe I do.

BEN. You do?

BEATRIZ. Maybe...small explosions...

BEN. But explosions nonetheless...

BEATRIZ. Maybe...

BEN. *(beat)* Maybe me too.

BEATRIZ. *(a smile)* But maybe it is the Fanta...

(She chuckles. Sees a letter on Ben's desk.)

BEATRIZ. From your mother? Another letter?

BEN. She just wants to know how I am...

BEATRIZ. Have you written her about me?

BEN. *(no)* Well...

BEATRIZ. Oh...

BEN. No it's –

BEATRIZ. Are you ashamed?

BEN. NO, Beatriz –

BEATRIZ. Then why –

BEN. Listen – my mother has always so wanted me to meet someone, to be happy – and I've never had the chance to bring a girl home to meet her, a girl I love –

BEATRIZ. Then why...?

BEN. Because there's nothing I want more than to see my mother's face when I tell her how unbelievably happy you make me feel.

BEATRIZ. *(a smile)* Good answer.

(Lights down.)

Scene 2

(The Commission continues. **BISHOP MELINDA** *is questioning* **CESAR**.*)*

BISHOP MELINDA. So what happened after you took him to Nueva Santa Isabela?

CESAR. I call Gonzalez –

BISHOP MELINDA. You are referring to Colonel Raul Gonzalez, of the Rebel Union Front?

CESAR. Yes, I tell him here there is an American. He should look at him.

BISHOP MELINDA. Why?

CESAR. Perhaps he is CIA, working with the army.

BISHOP MELINDA. So what did you do?

CESAR. There is a boy under Gonzalez' command who is sick all of the time, Diego is his name. So Gonzalez sends him to the doctor. And they watch him...

BISHOP MELINDA. What did they find out?

CESAR. That he is a good doctor. That is all they find. So they stop watching him.

BISHOP MELINDA. And then...?

CESAR. Months later the doctor telephones me. He is going to the airport, going home to United States the next morning, he asks me to drive him. He pays in dollars so...I pick him up in Nueva Santa Isabela...and there is something not right...

BISHOP MELINDA. What was that?

CESAR. His things. His bags. He has very little with him, you see.

BISHOP MELINDA. Why is that strange?

CESAR. A man does not travel away from home with many things and return home with little. It is not right.

BISHOP MELINDA. Did you talk on the way to the airport?

CESAR. No. He is quiet. He only looks out the window. There is a sadness. *(beat)* We go to the airport, he pays a good tip and that is all. I go home, to sleep. Until Gonzalez telephones me.

BISHOP MELINDA. Why did he call you?

CESAR. Because the doctor is seen at the *mercado* on Calle Ramirez. He is still in Cartuga. Gonzalez knows something is not right – the doctor goes to the airport with almost nothing, says he leaves Cartuga only to remain – and he stays in Cartuga City – at the *mercado* – and the *mercado* is only a kilometer from army headquarters. Everything fits together.

BISHOP MELINDA. What did?

CESAR. That he is CIA, working with the army. For this there is only one answer.

BISHOP MELINDA. What...?

CESAR. Gonzalez says we must remove the doctor.

BISHOP MELINDA. *(beat)* What did you do?

CESAR. Drive my cab to the *mercado*. Wait for him. He appears with a package. A package he did not have with him before.

BISHOP MELINDA. How did you know this was not medical supplies?

CESAR. It is too small. No, this is something else. Papers, Bishop. Lists perhaps. Of those who are to disappear. *La Panel Negra.* The army takes lives. Gonzalez, he says he too can take lives. *Venganza.*

BISHOP MELINDA. Revenge.

CESAR. The doctor asks me if I would not mind to take him to Nueva Santa Isabela.

BISHOP MELINDA. Did you take Dr. Montgomery to Nueva Santa Isabela?

CESAR. No.

BISHOP MELINDA. Where did you take him?

CESAR. We turn off the road before Nueva Santa Isabela, after Peletan. We are met by Gonzalez and the men.

BISHOP MELINDA. What then?

CESAR. I give them the doctor and the package and I go.

BISHOP MELINDA. You did not take part in what happened next?

CESAR. No, this is not something I do. I drive. I give information, for Paco. But not...*(beat; pained)* I am not a coward, Bishop...but I do not pull the trigger.

(Pause.)

BISHOP MELINDA. Do you know what happened to Dr. Montgomery?

CESAR. Yes. Gonzalez telephones me the next day.

BISHOP MELINDA. What did he say?

CESAR. They take him down to the caves. Gonzalez says the doctor is very frightened – begging for his life. Gonzalez laughs when...

BISHOP MELINDA. When what?

CESAR. *(beat)* When he smells piss on the man.

BISHOP MELINDA. *(pause)* Continue...

CESAR. They enter the mouth of the cave. Shine a light on the doctor. He cries I think. *(beat)* Then they shoot him four times.

*(**BENJAMIN SR.** jumps up –)*

BENJAMIN SR. YOU SICK –

BISHOP MELINDA. Mr. Montgomery, please.

*(**BENJAMIN SR.** slowly sits, still enraged.)*

CESAR. One bullet for each decade of military rule. He is dead then. They put the body in the river.

BENJAMIN SR. He was a doctor. That's all he was.

CESAR. *(to **BISHOP MELINDA**)* It is only later, much later, that we learn he is not CIA, not working with the army...we do not know this then.

BENJAMIN SR. He was innocent.

BISHOP MELINDA. Mr. Montgomery –

CESAR. *(to **BENJAMIN SR.**)* He is innocent? – *todos son inocente* – all of us – we are all victims.

BENJAMIN SR. That doesn't justify murder!

CESAR. I do nothing wrong.

BENJAMIN SR. You killed my son! You go to hell!

CESAR. Only God can decide this – not you.

BISHOP MELINDA. Please, everyone, let us –

CESAR. You have no right to judge me – you do not live here –

BENJAMIN SR. *You* have no right –

CESAR. You do not have to endure to survive like we do – Gonzalez, me, Diego, we fight for our home –

BENJAMIN SR. He did nothing to you – and you murdered him –

BISHOP MELINDA. Mr. Montgomery – Mr. Santos –

BENJAMIN SR. You are a *murderer* –

CESAR. Only my people can judge me – and when this is over they will tell me to go home – not to prison –

BISHOP MELINDA. *(pleading) Can we have order please?*

CESAR. Because back then it is a war – and there is casualties.

BISHOP MELINDA. Please – *PLEASE* –

(Lights cut out.)

Scene 3

*(Ben's examination room. **BEN** enters without a key, closes the door. Locks it.)*

BEN. Hello? Beatriz?

*(**BEATRIZ** pops out from underneath the desk. She is scared.)*

BEN. There you are. What were you doing under the desk?

BEATRIZ. So I would be out of view. Where were you? You said you would be here earlier.

BEN. I know, I – *(notices her fear)* – Beatriz, what's wrong?

BEATRIZ. This morning, Ben –

BEN. What is it? Why are you shaking?

BEATRIZ. *(trying to say something difficult)* My mentor, Carlos...

BEN. Yes –

BEATRIZ. Ben, he was taken today.

BEN. What?

BEATRIZ. *La Panel Negra.*

BEN. The Black Van?

(she nods.)

BEN. He was taken?

BEATRIZ. Made to disappear.

BEN. How do you –

BEATRIZ. It was in broad daylight – a woman saw, she knew him, she told the department at the university...in broad daylight...never to be seen again.

BEN. Oh my God, I'm so sorry. Are you okay?

BEATRIZ. I was told about Carlos at lunch. When I got home...

BEN. What? What happened?

BEATRIZ. A man was waiting.

BEN. Who? What man?

BEATRIZ. I did not know him. He had a warning for me. The same one he delivered to Carlos.

BEN. Oh God.

BEATRIZ. I do not know what to do, Ben – I have to run – hide in the hills –

BEN. You can't live like that –

BEATRIZ. It is the only way –

BEN. Wait – before you do that –

BEATRIZ. *(hostile, on edge)* What?

BEN. Alright, calm down.

BEATRIZ. Calm down? My teacher was kidnapped today, Ben! My life was threatened!

BEN. I know – listen...have a Fanta.

BEATRIZ. What?

BEN. Just have a Fanta.

BEATRIZ. I do not want a Fanta!

BEN. You'll catch your breath and then we can think this out. Please.

(He gets her a Fanta, opens it, hands it to her. She takes it.)

BEN. Have some.

(She drinks.)

BEN. Okay. Now sit down. Okay?

(She sits on the examination table.)

BEN. Now. Here's the thing – don't react crazy just hear me out, okay? – I think there is a solution to this and the solution is –

BEATRIZ. What?

BEN. Come home with me.

BEATRIZ. Leave Cartuga?

BEN. My visa runs out in two weeks. I have to go back. Come with me. You're in danger here.

BEATRIZ. My work is here, Ben. I cannot stop – this is who I am...

BEN. But –

BEATRIZ. Why did you come here? It was because you believed, yes?

BEN. Yes, of course –

BEATRIZ. Well *I* believe, Ben.

BEN. *(beat; admiring)* I know you do...but you can't help any peasants if you're dead, Beatriz.

BEATRIZ. I cannot help them in the United States.

BEN. Yes you can. Work on their behalf, educate people on what's going on – my mother is in politics, she can help you – are you kidding, she would *love* to help – there's so much you can do there.

BEATRIZ. My family...

BEN. Your family wants you safe. *(beat)* I want you safe. *(beat)* Come with me.

(She's considering...)

BEATRIZ. I would not be let out of the country.

BEN. Okay, true but...is there a way to get to Mexico? Through the jungle?

BEATRIZ. It is possible...

BEN. Then it's possible for us to get to Mexico City and go to the U.S. embassy and seek asylum.

BEATRIZ. But I have heard stories of those who have tried. Even if they did make it through the jungle, they were turned away by the embassies in Mexico City. And then the Cartugan army found out.

BEN. But we'd be together, I'd make sure –

BEATRIZ. No –

BEN. What, no? Why not?

BEATRIZ. You go back home, where it is safe.

BEN. But you're not safe here.

BEATRIZ. What if...*(beat)* What if I went through the jungle. Alone. I could make it.

BEN. Alone? I couldn't do that –

BEATRIZ. I can make it on my own. I know the land, I know the people. I can move faster alone. You would attract attention.

BEN. But –

BEATRIZ. And you could go home and make arrangements with the embassy for me, for when I arrive in Mexico City. So they would be expecting me, so I would not be turned away. Could you do that?

BEN. Sure, my mother knows people in the State Department, but Beatriz –

BEATRIZ. Ben – you must trust me.

BEN. I don't know. *(beat)* Are you sure?

BEATRIZ. This is the best way. *(beat)* Would I...have a home in the United States?

BEN. Oh my God, my mom would love you. And you could do your work there. Where it's safe. Please come.

BEATRIZ. It's so far away...

(He takes her hand.)

BEN. Do you love me?

BEATRIZ. *(beat; then looks up at him)* Yes.

BEN. Will you come?

BEATRIZ. *(beat)* Yes.

(Lights down.)

Scene 4

(The Commission. **BISHOP MELINDA** *is finishing with* **CESAR**.*)*

BISHOP MELINDA. I have just one more question. Colonel Gonzalez, do you know where he is?

CESAR. He is in the hills somewhere. Who knows now the fighting is over.

BISHOP MELINDA. You do not know his whereabouts?

CESAR. Guatemala? Peru? Who knows this?

BISHOP MELINDA. I see. *(beat)* Now I would like to turn the questioning over to the victim's family, if they so choose. Would you like to do so?

BENJAMIN SR. Yes I would.

BISHOP MELINDA. Please approach the microphone.

*(***BENJAMIN SR.*** rises, goes to a table with a microphone.)*

BENJAMIN SR. For the *record*, because I'm not sure that this is the *focus* of this proceeding – *(to* **CESAR***)* My son is *dead*, you son of a bitch –

BISHOP MELINDA. Mr. Montgomery –

BENJAMIN SR. You sick –

BISHOP MELINDA. Please! Do you have a question for Mr. Santos, Mr. Montgomery?

BENJAMIN SR. No I don't. I'm going to make *my* statement now, thank you. *(beat)* Let me tell you something, *(with disgust)* Mr. Santos. And this is for you, Bishop. And for those in the audience and those listening in and all the cameras – I want you all to understand the definition of injustice. Because that is what is happening here today. And it makes me sick.

BISHOP MELINDA. Please, this is a civil commiss –

BENJAMIN SR. I'm not finished, Bishop. I waited my turn. I'm the only one here who apparently finds fault with your little commission. So naive. "Build the future based on a shared memory." *Memory* isn't bringing my son back. And memory sure isn't going to punish this man who killed him. Where I'm from we don't *announce* a man's guilt and then let him *free*. What that *is* is called *injustice*. Plain and simple. It is taking a wrong and condoning it. And it is unconscionable for you, Bishop, to sit perched on your throne and allow this to happen.

BISHOP MELINDA. The church denounces all wrongs, we always have –

BENJAMIN SR. Oh really? I guess we have conveniently forgotten about the inquisition. Now who's talking about a shared memory? *(beat)* You think that anytime there is conflict and abuse like apartheid in South Africa or oppression here or maybe slavery in my country that you can just cart out your traveling Truth and Reconciliation Commission, roll out the country's Bishop Tutu and publish a report and that solves the problem. That solves nothing. You can't compromise justice with truth. As if we could possibly know the truth anyway. You speak of it as if it's something that can be calculated, like how many oranges you have in a basket. X equals the truth. As if we could ever *really* know.

(beat) You speak about creating an environment for reconciliation. What you are doing is solidifying an environment for impunity.

You want to move forward, here's how you do it: show the citizens of this country that a wrong is a wrong and wrongs get punished. That this country is not tolerating abuses anymore. That those that abuse – get punished. It's called a system of justice. And I'll tell you something – no one here's going to believe this place has changed until you show them that the days of injustice *are over*.

BISHOP MELINDA. We hope to achieve justice through reconciliation – an enriched form of justice.

BENJAMIN SR. *(passionate)* This commission cannot force reconciliation! Because reconciliation follows forgiveness. And ONLY I CAN FORGIVE. Me. Alone. And I DO NOT forgive. *(pause; then to* **CESAR***)* You talk about your brother's murder. I say this to you: any innocent man with a heart whose family was killed would not do the same to another innocent man. You are a bad man. *You* deserve to be shot four times in the dark with a bright light shining in *your* face. *You* deserve to be dumped in a river like garbage.

(pause) And you, Bishop, the moral compass of the community, refusing to take a position on the morality of killing another human being. When you sacrifice that, you sacrifice *all* morality. Because there can be *no truth* without acknowledging that a wrong was committed, and that someone is *responsible*. When you refuse to do that, when you *compromise the truth*, then the truth you've created is, in reality, *a lie*. And when your truth is a lie, Bishop – then so is your so-called reconciliation.

BISHOP MELINDA. *(trying to contain himself)* Do you have any questions, Mr. Montgomery?

BENJAMIN SR. I'm done here.

*(***BENJAMIN SR.*** walks away in disgust.)*

LYNNE. *(rising)* I do. I want to say something.

BISHOP MELINDA. If you feel up to it, Mrs. Montgomery.

LYNNE. I do.

BISHOP MELINDA. Please...

*(She walks by **BENJAMIN SR.** and goes to the microphone.)*

BISHOP MELINDA. Please, Mrs. Montgomery, whenever you are ready...

*(She takes a few moments to silently gather herself before she is ready. Then she looks up at **CESAR**. Her voice is filled with loss but not rage.)*

LYNNE. Are you a religious man, Mr. Santos?

CESAR. I am.

LYNNE. What religion are you?

CESAR. Catholic.

LYNNE. Me too. *(pause; this is not necessarily directed at Cesar)* When I was a girl my grandmother would sit me on her lap while I held her rosary. When Ben was a boy he would play with that same rosary, he could just sit for hours on the carpet with the rosary, and I would have to tell him it wasn't a toy. I found myself sounding remarkably like my grandmother. *(beat)* When I came here this week...I brought that rosary with me.

(Pause.)

BISHOP MELINDA. Mrs. Montgomery, are you alright?

LYNNE. *(gathering herself again)* Yes. *(beat)* Mr. Santos...do you know why, Ben didn't get on his plane? Did he tell you?

CESAR. No, I do not know this. He only smiles and asks to go to Nueva Santa Isabela.

LYNNE. *(surprised)* He was smiling?

CESAR. Yes.

LYNNE. Do you know why?

CESAR. *(shakes his head no)* He holds his package and smiles, like a boy on his birthday.

LYNNE. He was happy.

CESAR. Yes.

LYNNE. *(a relief)* Thank you.

(Beat.)

BISHOP MELINDA. Is that all, Mrs. Montgomery?

LYNNE. I think...no, actually. I'd like to make a statement. May I make a statement?

BISHOP MELINDA. Of course.

LYNNE. *(pause; thinks)* I flew here from America to find out what happened to my Ben, and why....It's a beautiful country here...but a country that had been made ugly. I can't tell you how to heal your country. I just know a lot of families were torn apart. Because the army was killing and *(looks at* **CESAR***)* your guerillas were killing. Everyone was killing, except for those who didn't have any guns. They just prayed they wouldn't get killed. Maybe, if you're really lucky, after many, many years, the pain from losing loved ones will heal a little. Maybe even enough to change things around here.

(beat; to **CESAR***)* I'm sorry what happened to your family. You have a right to feel angry. After what you've been through, what you've had taken from you, after what you believed about Ben, what seemed so clear...

(beat) Still...you took a *life*, my *son's life* – you took it like it meant nothing. *(beat)* Ben wasn't a threat or a symbol or a pawn or a statistic. He was Ben. He was Ben who every Christmas got a new Star Wars figure. *(slight chuckle)* Even in high school. He was Ben who visited his grandfather even when his grandfather couldn't recognize him any longer, and Ben would just sit by him and hold his hand and make a lonely man feel not so alone for a little while. He was Ben who believed in something bigger than himself. He was Ben my son. My beautiful son. And when you took him from me you tore my heart right out. *(beat)* You can't bring him back, Mr. Santos. *(beat)* I can't either. I can't tell him that I love him. And miss him. That I'm – that I'm sorry I taught him to try to do the right thing, because it meant going to a place that would take him away from me. That I want nothing else in this world other than for him to get on that plane. *(beat)* That's my torture. *(beat)* You took his life. And if you have any goodness in you at all, then that is your torture.

(**LYNNE** *rises and walks towards the door. As she passes* **BENJAMIN SR.***, he puts his arm out to touch her but she pulls away, then walks out. He gets up and follows her as* **BISHOP MELINDA** *speaks:*)

BISHOP MELINDA. Mr. Santos, the commission will continue interviewing in order to verify your statements and if they are found to be the entire truth then it will grant your request of amnesty.

(**CESAR** *silently nods.*)

BISHOP MELINDA. This session of the Commission is adjourned.

(And the lights come down on the Truth Commission and rise on another part of the stage. **LYNNE** *enters.* **BENJAMIN SR.** *catches up with her.)*

BENJAMIN SR. Are you okay?

LYNNE. No I am not okay and it has nothing to do with a man not being executed in retaliation.

BENJAMIN SR. It's what he deserves.

LYNNE. Do you think it's what Ben would have wanted?

(Beat.)

LYNNE. This is about *our son* – don't you see?! – our *(it's hard to get out)* dead...son.

BENJAMIN SR. *(an explosion)* Don't you think I know that! *(beat; calming)* You don't think I think of Ben? A classroom full of students who look just like him and I don't think of him?

LYNNE. *(really asking)* Do you?

BENJAMIN SR. *(pained)* Everyday.

LYNNE. This never goes away, does it?

*(****BENJAMIN SR.*** *slowly starts to cry. It overtakes him.)*

BENJAMIN SR. Please forgive me. Forgive me. Please. I didn't tell him not to go.

*(****LYNNE*** *is taken aback, not expecting this. She touches him, looks into his eyes.)*

LYNNE. Benjamin. I didn't either.

(And in that moment: they forgive each other.)

LYNNE. Every time I look at you I see Ben. You have the same eyes, you know. The same blue eyes. There's something comforting about looking into your eyes. *(beat)* Benjamin... is there an "us" without Ben? Because I can't remember an "us" without Ben.

BENJAMIN SR. Can we just...leave this place? Go back home. Sort things out. We can keep the attic the way it is. If that helps. However you want it. We can go to the airport right now. Be home faster than you can imagine. Now that it's over.

LYNNE. But it's not.

BENJAMIN SR. There's nothing left here –

LYNNE. Why did he go to the *mercado*?

BENJAMIN SR. What?

LYNNE. Ben. Instead of getting on the plane. Why do you think he did that?

BENJAMIN SR. I don't know. Can I get a car? To take us to the airport?

LYNNE. I can't leave.

BENJAMIN SR. What – why?

LYNNE. Not until I go there.

BENJAMIN SR. To the *mercado*?

LYNNE. Not until I find the whole truth.

BENJAMIN SR. You're chasing after a ghost, Lynne.

LYNNE. We both are.

BENJAMIN SR. *(beat; an acceptance)* When will I see you again?

LYNNE. I don't know. When I'm ready to say goodbye.

BENJAMIN SR. *(stricken)* To me?

LYNNE. No...not you...

(A moment, and then he understands.)

BENJAMIN SR. I can come with you.

*(**LYNNE** takes his hand, holds it tenderly, shakes her head no. This is something she must do. He gets it.)*

BENJAMIN SR. I'll be at the hotel.

(She goes. Lights fade.)

Scene 5

(Ben's examination room. He has packed up the supplies and put them in a large box on the desk. A small box is on the table. A small suitcase is near the door. **BEN** *removes his white coat with much care, then lays it across the chair. Door knock.)*

BEATRIZ. *(cheery)* Doctor Ben...

BEN. Come in.

*(***BEATRIZ*** comes in. She looks radiant.)*

BEN. Wow.

BEATRIZ. What?

BEN. You look stunning.

BEATRIZ. This is the last time you see me so...

*(***BEN*** doesn't feel comfortable with that.)*

BEN. Has everything been okay today? No strangers following you or anything?

BEATRIZ. No. Please do not worry.

BEN. Every day that you are here is a worry.

BEATRIZ. Tonight I have my final meeting with the *campesinos*, then I can leave from Nueva Santa Isabela tomorrow after dinner. No one will suspect.

BEN. Do you have to meet with them?

BEATRIZ. I cannot abandon them without a plan of communication. This you must understand.

BEN. I do, it's just...of course I do. Listen, the thing is, I've been doing some thinking and –

BEATRIZ. Ben, we have talked about it.

BEN. I know – I know, but I just – two are better than one, aren't they? I mean, you could get injured and no one would find you.

BEATRIZ. I will not get injured.

BEN. It happens all the time. To experienced hikers. And I could help. I'm a doctor!

BEATRIZ. Ben, I can do it.

BEN. Don't say that just to protect me. I want to come with you.

BEATRIZ. I know you do. I will be okay. I have all the information – maps of this area, how to get to the U.S. embassy in Mexico City, your phone number and address in America....There are very few soldiers up that far north so do not worry about me. Go home to your family. It will be only a week.

(**BEN** *is torn.*)

BEN. *(pointing to the small box on the table)* Well at least take this.

BEATRIZ. What is it?

BEN. It's a medical care package I made for you. *(going through it)* There's tigan, for nausea and vomiting; larium, which is anti-malarial – technically, you should have started taking it two weeks ago but go ahead and take one now – *(he gives her one and she takes it)* – cephalexin, it's an antibiotic –

BEATRIZ. Ben –

BEN. – some benadryl, for allergic reactions; bacitracin and tape, for cuts; and some viper anti-venom – it won't work for all snakes, just vipers, but it was all I had so if you get bitten by a snake...I guess just hope it's a viper.

BEATRIZ. Ben.

BEN. Yes?

BEATRIZ. I will be okay. I promise.

BEN. Okay. Just take it with you. Just in case. It would make me feel better.

(*She takes it.*)

BEATRIZ. Do you have your plane ticket?

BEN. Yeah, in my pocket.

BEATRIZ. How are you getting to the airport?

BEN. I called a driver I know. The dirt roads will be difficult at night so we're giving ourselves a lot of time.

BEATRIZ. Look at you. You know my home so well now.

BEN. Soon you'll know mine.

BEATRIZ. When does the driver arrive?

BEN. He'll be here any minute.

BEATRIZ. *(sadly)* Oh...

BEN. I'm going to miss you so much.

BEATRIZ. Just don't think of me...

BEN. I can't do that.

BEATRIZ. *(a smile)* Good. Everything will be fine, as long as no one becomes suspicious. You told no one about us, right?

BEN. Right.

BEATRIZ. Me, too. It is hard. I want to shout it. The town – they will miss you, too. You helped so many people.

BEN. I'm glad.

BEATRIZ. They are grateful. And now – the clothing...

BEN. You heard about that?

BEATRIZ. How can I not? Everywhere are people walking around in your things – overnight the town is full of fans of the Baltimore Orioles.

BEN. They need it more than I do.

BEATRIZ. So this is your suitcase?

BEN. That's it.

BEATRIZ. It is so small. This is all you take back home with you?

BEN. No. Something else.

(He puts his arms around her. The sound of a car honking.)

BEN. Oh shit.

BEATRIZ. The driver?

BEN. *(calling out) Un momento...(to* **BEATRIZ***)* Beatriz, I don't – God I *hate* this.

BEATRIZ. Endings are –

BEN. This is *not* an ending.

BEATRIZ. I did not mean that.

BEN. This is a beginning, right? We'll see each other soon.

BEATRIZ. Soon – in the United States.

BEN. Even before that – I'll meet you in Mexico. And when I see you next I'll have chocolate. A big package of chocolate. That's *my* promise.

(Car horn again.)

BEN. Okay – I guess I should –

BEATRIZ. Wait, I have something for you.

BEN. What is it?

BEATRIZ. Among the Maya there is a legend of a princess who loved a man she was not allowed to love. The two were forced to separate, but were unable to live without one another. Heartbroken, the princess visited a shaman who, moved by her sorrow, turned her into a beetle that sparkled as if covered in gems – *a piece of living jewelry.* Her lover then pinned her to his heart, so she could be with him forever.

BEN. That's really beautiful.

BEATRIZ. The Maya make this piece of jewelry...

(BEATRIZ takes from her bag a large live beetle which has been decorated with rhinestones and is attached to a little gold chain leash [a clothespin]. She pins the leash to Ben's shirt, near his heart. The beetle sparkles as it wanders aimlessly about a small portion of Ben's shirt.)

BEN. *(a chuckle)* I've never worn a piece of living jewelry...

BEATRIZ. Until you see me – this will be me. *(beat)* Now say goodbye.

BEN. How am I going to last a week without you, I can't make it two days without you.

BEATRIZ. *(demonstrates with her hand to the beetle)* Find your heart, and you will find me. Say goodbye.

BEN. Goodbye.

BEATRIZ. I love you, Ben.

BEN. I love you, Beatriz.

(Another car horn.)

BEN. I'd better –

BEATRIZ. Here.

(She gives him the suitcase. They kiss.)

BEN. One week...

BEATRIZ. One week...

BEN. *Una semana.*

(She smiles. And he exits. She sits on the examination table. It feels very alone in there all of a sudden.)

BEATRIZ. *Una semana.*

(Lights down.)

Scene 6

(**BEN** *is at a payphone at the airport. He holds his small suitcase in one hand and the plane ticket in the other. He looks pensive.*)

BEN. Mom, it's Ben – are you there? ...no? Okay. This is costing me a fortune so I'll be quick, my plane gets in at uhh... 6PM, at Dulles so...could you pick me up? What am I saying, of course you will...It's been, yeah it's been something and I have something to show you. It's wonderful. I can't wait....See you – wow, I'll see you tomorrow. *(beat)* Love you.

(*He hangs up the phone. Takes a step as if to go to the gate. Then stops. He looks down at the beetle jewelry. Touches it.*)

BEN. *(to himself)* It's wonderful...

(**BEN** *looks around him, thinks, his mind whirling. He makes a decision, throws the ticket away and walks in the direction away from the gate. We hear the sound of a plane taking off.*

LYNNE *enters another part of the stage; outside the mercado. It is a place of great activity. She stares offstage at it, a whirl of emotion.*

She presses play on the tape player.)

TAPE PLAYER. Mom, it's Ben – are yoooooooooooooooo——

(*Something's wrong – the tape player isn't working –*)

LYNNE. What? – no – no –

(*She frantically tries to fix it but nothing works –*)

LYNNE. No – please – please work – don't –

CESAR. *(offstage)* Mrs. Montgomery...?

(*She looks up.* **CESAR** *walks onstage.*)

CESAR. Are you alright?

LYNNE. What are you doing here?

CESAR. I follow you from the Commission.

LYNNE. Go away.

CESAR. Because you do not look well.

LYNNE. I know how I look.

CESAR. Is there something I can do? I think maybe you need some help.

LYNNE. I don't need your help.

CESAR. Please...I am not a bad man...

(Beat.)

CESAR. *(re: tape player)* Is it this? *(his hand out, asking to take it)* Please...? I know these machines.

(Beat. She reluctantly hands him the tape player. He examines it for a moment.)

CESAR. It is broken.

LYNNE. Thanks.

CESAR. But the tape is safe. We are beside the *mercado* – I know a man who sells these – it will take only a moment. Please.

(He runs offstage in the direction of the mercado.

Just as – **BEN** *appears, exiting the mercado, walking right past* **LYNNE***, who does not see him. He is looking around, taking in his surroundings, smiling, carrying his small suitcase and now carrying a package [the same kind he had in the examination room earlier – that contained chocolate]. There is a purpose to his movements.*

He spots **CESAR***, who is waiting by the car for* **BEN** *to exit the mercado. There is something dark about* **CESAR** *– he knows what he has to do.)*

CESAR. *Que tal, amigo.*

BEN. Cesar! My old friend! What are you doing here by the *mercado?*

CESAR. What are *you* doing here? You have a plane, yes?

BEN. I did, yeah...

CESAR. What happened?

BEN. I was at the airport and they were announcing the flight and...and I just realized I couldn't leave. I didn't want to.

CESAR. What is it you do in the *mercado, amigo*?

BEN. I bought a gift.

CESAR. *(not buying it)* For who?

BEN. *(stops)* Oh, no one. I can't say. Just a friend. No one really.

CESAR. I see.

BEN. Listen – I need to get to Nueva Santa Isabela by dinnertime. Can you get me there? I mean are you free?

CESAR. Of course.

BEN. That's great. It's so funny you're here. You're like my guardian angel in Cartuga. *(beat)* Oh – but I should call my mother first.

(**BEN** *looks around for a phone.*)

CESAR. *(pointing)* But there is a long line for the phone.

BEN. I'm kind of in a hurry...

CESAR. You can call when you reach Nueva Santa Isabela, no?

BEN. Umm – yeah, I guess that would be fine.

CESAR. All that money for a plane ticket and then...not on the plane, huh...?

BEN. Yeah...couldn't leave...

CESAR. And now...back to Nueva Santa Isabela...

BEN. *(excited)* Yeah...and then home.

CESAR. *(indicating package and small suitcase)* And this is all you take home with you?

BEN. *(a smile)* No.

CESAR. I see. *(beat; as if to put it in the trunk)* I take this?

BEN. No, no, I'll hold on to it.

(**CESAR** *nods knowingly. Lights fade on* **BEN**. **CESAR** *returns to* **LYNNE** *from the mercado with a new tape player and the tape.*)

CESAR. I believe this fits correctly. *(putting the tape into new* *tape player)* The man, he knows this is for you so he wants to charge American price but I say you are my friend and he charges local price. There.

(He presses play – and we hear Ben's voice. **LYNNE** *grabs the tape player from him, stops it immediately.)*

LYNNE. I'm not your friend.

CESAR. Do you need help? A doctor? Because I can find one for you if –

LYNNE. I don't need a doctor. I just want to go...

CESAR. Where...?

LYNNE. I don't –

CESAR. I will help – where do you want to go –

LYNNE. I don't know...where to go....I don't want to leave but I don't know where to go...

CESAR. Every year, I drive to Talaca, at night, in the darkness, to the place where my brother's remains rest...I lay a flower there...it is a small thing but to me it is not a small thing, you understand? Perhaps...you would like to lay a flower...?

LYNNE. A flower?

CESAR. At the place where your son rests. The caves. By Nueva Santa Isabela. Would you like to do this?

LYNNE. Yes. Yes, I think I would very much like to do that.

CESAR. It is far but. Will you allow me to take you?

LYNNE. No, I don't think so –

CESAR. My car is right here – *(he indicates stage right, where Ben was a moment ago)* – I will drive you, please allow me this. Mrs. Montgomery, your words at the Commission – I hear them. I do not feel wrong for helping to end a threat to my people but...I do feel...a torture... for taking your son. *(beat)* I also have a son. 16 months old. *Se llama Alejandro. (beat)* Please. I am trying to make amends.

(She looks at him.)

CESAR. Please.

(Lights down.)

Scene 7

(Lights rise on Cesar's car, with **BEN** *in the back seat holding his box.* **BEN** *is excited.)*

BEN. *(looking out the window and pointing)* That's bananas. That's sugar cane. *Caña.* And that's cotton over there, right?

*(***CESAR** *quietly nods in the front seat.)*

BEN. See, I know this area. I can do this. *(beat)* Cesar, have you ever been through the jungle?

CESAR. No. Why?

BEN. Just wondering...*(beat)* Have you ever eaten a termite?

CESAR. Yes.

BEN. Are they minty?

CESAR. Yes.

(Beat.)

BEN. Have you ever been in love, Cesar?

CESAR. What?

BEN. Do you have a wife, kids?

CESAR. *(beat)* I have a wife.

BEN. It's wonderful, isn't it? The most wonderful thing.

*(***CESAR** *steels himself.)*

CESAR. Almost there...

(Beat. **BEN** *continues looking out the window.)*

BEN. Hey! Is that a quetzal bird?!

CESAR. Where?

BEN. There! Wait, it flew off.

CESAR. Are you sure, not everyday you see quetzal.

BEN. Yeah. Wow, its colors were stunning.

*(***CESAR** *turns the car onto a different road. The turn caught* **BEN** *off guard, and the package he is holding moves, causing the beetle leash to become undone. The beetle falls to the floor of the cab.)*

BEN. My beetle jewelry...it fell...*(he looks up)* Wait...Cesar, isn't Nueva Santa Isabela a few minutes still down that road?

CESAR. *(beat)* Yes.

BEN. But you turned...

CESAR. Shortcut.

BEN. Oh this must be near the caves. I always wanted to see the caves.

(BEN goes down to find the jewelry. CESAR looks determined. Then a light change in the back seat. CESAR remains lit.

Lights come up on the back of the car and now LYNNE is there instead of BEN. She is listening to the tape player.)

TAPE PLAYER. *(Ben's voice)* See you – wow, I'll see you tomorrow. *(beat)* Love you. *(click)*

LYNNE. Love you...

(She turns it off. There is a moment of silence. She looks out the window, puts the tape player down.)

CESAR. You do not play it again?

LYNNE. No.

CESAR. May I ask – do you have other tapes of your son, Mrs. Montgomery?

LYNNE. Many. At home.

CESAR. At many ages?

LYNNE. Yes. Why?

CESAR. Why do you play this one?

LYNNE. What?

CESAR. If you have all those tapes of him, why is it this one that you play?

LYNNE. *(beat)* As a reminder.

(Beat.)

CESAR. I wish I could have a tape of my brother. *(pause)* I am thinking right now after the events of today...and I am wondering if Paco would want it to be that a man is dead for him...I do not think he would want this...

(Pause.)

CESAR. It is only five more minutes to the caves.

*(**LYNNE** nods silently. Beat.)*

CESAR. Your son...that day...*te queria llamar...*

LYNNE. What?

CESAR. Before we leave, that final trip, he wants to call you. But, you see, there is a line for the phone.

LYNNE. Oh.

CESAR. I want you to know.

LYNNE. I could have had one more conversation with him... *(beat)*...I would give anything in the world....

CESAR. We cannot wait for the phone because we must hurry, he says, get to Nueva Santa Isabela before dinnertime.

LYNNE. Why would he be in such a rush?

CESAR. He does not say.

LYNNE. I mean...other than work, right? A patient?

CESAR. I do not know another reason.

LYNNE. That must be why he didn't get on the plane. It's what I taught him, to do the right thing.

CESAR. Do not feel a burden. He helps many people in the town. He is a good doctor.

LYNNE. But...then why did they kill him? I mean, if they thought he was CIA or working with the army, couldn't they have questioned him, even tortured him or – I don't know – but they would have *learned*, they would have *known* there was no way possible that Ben was *anything* but a doctor...

CESAR. There are things that do not concern your son...

LYNNE. I came here for answers...will you tell me?

CESAR. *(beat)* Normally they might interrogate, yes, but...

LYNNE. But what?

CESAR. Something happens the night your son leaves Nueva Santa Isabela....there is a university student...a woman who helps many peasants in the town...who is leaving a meeting with these very *campesinos*...and after the meeting, a little boy, Diego, sees *La Panel Negra*, the black van, he sees it take her...*desaparecio* – the van makes her disappear, you see...gone. A girl who does nothing but try to show *campesinos* how to work the land and organize...*(beat)*...and it seems...it seems so *interesting*, you see, that your son leaves the night of her disappearance and returns the day after...

LYNNE. So it was because this woman was taken...that's the revenge you spoke about....Did my son know her?

CESAR. Your son knows only the inside of the church.

LYNNE. He must have been so lonely...

(Pause.)

CESAR. Mrs. Montgomery...?

LYNNE. Yes.

CESAR. I would like to give you something...

LYNNE. What's that?

CESAR. Long after your son is gone I find something in my car. Long after I learn the truth about him. *(beat)* This...

(He picks up the beetle – now dead, but still sparkling – and hands it back to her. She takes it and stares at it in wonderment.)

LYNNE. What is this?

CESAR. It is a beetle. With rhinestones.

LYNNE. Why does it have a leash?

CESAR. It is once alive. Your son wears it.

LYNNE. He wore a live beetle?

CESAR. There is a legend among the Maya. I cannot recall it all...but it concerns a woman who longs for a man she can no longer see...

LYNNE. Yes...?

CESAR. One of them is turned into a beetle so that the beetle can be worn on the breast of the other – and be near the other's heart forever.

(Pause.)

LYNNE. That's very beautiful.

*(**LYNNE** pins the beetle to her blouse, near her heart.)*

LYNNE. Ben told me he had something to show me. Something wonderful. Do you think...do you think maybe this was it?

CESAR. Perhaps.

LYNNE. Yes. Yes, this must be it. He must have bought this for me. This wonderful souvenir. *(beat)* Thank you, Mr. Santos. Thank you for helping me find the truth.

CESAR. Please do not thank me. It is very uncomfortable.

(The car stops.)

CESAR. We are here.

LYNNE. This is the place.

(CESAR nods. LYNNE stares out the window a moment, and then she turns back to CESAR, thinking deeply about something.)

LYNNE. Mr. Santos, will you remember Ben? After years pass, will you remember what you did to him?

CESAR. I will.

LYNNE. I want to believe you.

(Beat. LYNNE takes the tape player and reaches it forward to CESAR.

He doesn't take it.)

CESAR. I do not think so, Mrs. Mont –

LYNNE. Please. I want you to have this.

CESAR. Why?

LYNNE. As a reminder.

(Pause. CESAR slowly reaches and takes the tape player. LYNNE looks out the window at the place Ben was taken.)

CESAR. I will wait here. Take all the time you would like.

(Beat.)

LYNNE. I'm ready.

(She steels herself, and then she opens the car door and goes out – and lights cut out.)

END OF PLAY

JUMP/CUT
Neena Beber

Full Length / Drama / 2m, 1f /

Three bright urbanites want to make their mark on the world. Paul, a master of irony and distance, is a hardworking film maker on the rise. His girlfriend Karen, a grad student, must get on with her thesis or find a life outside of academia. Dave, a life long buddy whose brilliance is being consumed by increasingly severe episodes of manic depression, is camping on Paul's couch. Paul and Karen decide to turn Paul into a documentary. The camera is on 24 hours a day, capturing up close images of his jags and torpors and their responses. How far will love, friendship and ambition take this hip trio?

"Could not be more timely...
Fearlessly dives into provocative issues and ideas."
- *Washington Times*

"Savvy, solid play... about our fascination with victims and voyeurism, ...friendship and ambition, striving and its worth. Beber builds her characters... carefully with efficient and graceful layers of personalities and ideas... An accomplished piece of work structurally sound, snappily written and shot though with humor."
- *Washington City Paper*

"Fresh and compelling... clever and witty."
- *Arlington Weekly News*

"A sharp, funny, heartbreaking play that just pulls you in."
- *Montgomery Community Television*

"Quick and sharp... [with] something to say about the emotional environment we live in."
- *The Georgetowner*

"A remarkable, absorbing, complex and intelligent play."
- *Variety*

Winner of the L. Arnold Weissberger Award

SAMUELFRENCH.COM